A simple guide to

Common Worship

A simple guide to
Common Worship

*Introducing the new services
in your church*

Dana Delap
&
Gareth Lloyd

CANTERBURY
PRESS
Norwich

Extracts from *Common Worship: Services and Prayers for the Church of England* are copyright © The Archbishops' Council 2000 and are reproduced by permission.

Copyright © Dana Delap & Garth Lloyd 2000

First published in 2000 by The Canterbury Press Norwich (a publishing imprint of Hymns Ancient & Modern Limited a registered charity)
St Mary's Works, St Mary's Plain
Norwich, Norfolk NR3 3BH

British Library Cataloguing in Publication Data

A catalogue record for this book is available from the British Library

ISBN 1-85311-373-5

Printed in Great Britain by
Cox & Wyman Ltd, Reading, Berkshire

Contents

Acknowledgements

This book owes a great deal to the hard work of the Durham Diocesan Liturgical Team, led by Dana Delap. We would like to thank the other members of the Team – Nick Watson, David Kennedy, Nigel Stock, and Anna de Lange – for their encouragement.

The Diocesan Liturgical Committee have supported us in this venture, and they, with many others, have contributed to the introduction of *Common Worship* in the diocese and to this material in its various incarnations. Particular thanks go to Bruce Carlin, Anne Harrison, Tom Jamieson, David Stephenson, David Glover, Ben Gordon-Taylor, Paul Allinson, Gary Stott, James Lancelot, and Dominic Barrington. We are grateful to John Atherton for his kindness and for the enthusiasm of his welcomes, and to the churches and individuals in the diocese who have welcomed us so generously.

Our families, Adrian, Brigid and Miles, and Elizabeth and Jonathan, know more about liturgy than is good for them, and we therefore dedicate this book to them.

COLOURMASTER
INTERNATIONAL

PAD 21

THE BEACH AT ROCK, NR. PADSTOW PT128

Photo Precision Limited, St. Ives, Huntingdon

Dear Stephen,
Many happy return!
Here is a small thing
which may be useful
sometime (if it works!)
Much love Grandpa B.

January
1987

Midland Bank Group

in Britain and around the World

Christmas Eve, and twelve of the clock.
    'Now they are all on their knees',
An elder said as we sat in a flock
    By the embers in hearthside ease . . .

So fair a fancy few would weave
    In these years! Yet, I feel,
If someone said on Christmas Eve,
    'Come; see the oxen kneel

In the lonely barton by yonder coomb
    Our childhood used to know',
I should go with him in the gloom,
    Hoping it might be so.

Thomas Hardy, from *The Oxen*

Thomas Hardy (detail)
William Strang, 1920
Glasgow Art Gallery
& Museum

The authors

DANA DELAP is Development Officer for Introducing *Common Worship* in the Diocese of Durham.

Dana read Theology at St John's College, Durham, and has an MA in Applied Social Studies and a Diploma in Social Work. As pastoral assistant at St Peter's Church, Monkwearmouth, she was involved in the liturgical life of the parish, particularly in the experimental use of draft *Common Worship* materials. In her current post, Dana has developed a training programme and resources to introduce the new liturgy to the diocese.

She is married with two children aged 6 and 4, and lives within earshot of the Cathedral bells in Durham.

GARETH LLOYD is Vicar of Birtley in the Diocese of Durham, and Secretary of the Diocesan Liturgical Committee.

Gareth read Physics at King's College, Cambridge, and worked in electronics before beginning theological training in 1985. While priest-in-charge of St Peter's Church, Monkwearmouth in the 1990s, he developed a strong interest in pastoral liturgy. He recently completed a PhD on the process and mechanisms of liturgical reform in the Church of England during the twentieth century.

He is married with a 7-year-old son, with whom he converses fluently in their native Welsh tongue.

Preface

A Simple Guide to Common Worship is intended to help parishes during the early stages of using the new liturgy.

The new services are much more than simply the successors of the ASB; they embody a subtly different approach to worship, and offer far richer possibilities for pastoral care and for mission. To get the most out of *Common Worship*, parishes will need to give careful thought to the ethos of the new rites and how they can best be celebrated.

The material in this book has developed through a series of training events in the Diocese of Durham to introduce *Common Worship*. Over the last two years, we have found that the same questions keep recurring, and have therefore begun this book with a set of 'frequently asked questions'.

The rest of the book describes each of the new services and offers suggestions for using them effectively. We have tried to keep the material concise and readable, so that it will be useful to members of parish worship teams as well as being a resource to clergy and readers.

Finally, there is a substantial list of resources and further reading, and a simple glossary of terms.

1
Frequently Asked Questions about *Common Worship*

WHAT IS *COMMON WORSHIP*?

WHAT SORT OF BOOK ARE WE BEING OFFERED?

HOW WILL IT AFFECT OUR SUNDAY WORSHIP?

HOW DO WE MAKE THE CHANGE?

WHAT IS *COMMON WORSHIP*?

1 Why are the services changing?

Common Worship is the successor to the *Alternative Service Book* (ASB). A glance at the copyright page of an older copy of the ASB will show that the services were originally authorised until December 1990. The ASB was the final stage in a series of changes to the worship of the Church of England throughout the late 1960s and 1970s and, in order to give some stability to our liturgy, in 1985 General Synod extended the book's authorisation until 31 December 2000. Over the last twenty years the ASB has become a semi-permanent fixture, and a generation of Anglicans has known nothing else. No wonder the changeover to another set of services is proving challenging. However, both the language and the doctrinal emphasis of the ASB have dated, and *Common Worship* reflects the Church of England in a new century.

2 Why is it called *Common Worship*?

Some people have described *Common Worship* as 'variety worship', because so many options and commended resources are included, but each service has an accompanying Service Structure and Service Outline which make clear the shape of the service and the places where mandatory Church of England texts must be used. There is no doubt that the worship of the Church of England should be recognisable as such; local variety within an Anglican core.

3 Do churches have to use it?

The simple answer is, yes! *Common Worship* is authorised for use from 3 December 2000, and if a church wants to use modern language services, they must make the move to *Common Worship* by 1 January 2001. Diocesan bishops may give permission for churches to continue using the ASB for certain services (under the amended Canon B2) for up to two years, with possible extension for another three years. However, many diocesan bishops have made it clear that they are looking for a quick changeover to *Common Worship*.

The incumbent and PCC of each parish are required under Canon B3 to agree forms of service to be used in the benefice. This means that each PCC will have to resolve to use *Common Worship* in addition to the *Book of Common Prayer* (BCP). If the incumbent and PCC fail to agree, all services must be taken from the BCP. The PCC needs to pass something similar to the following motion

> 'This PCC resolves to adopt the provisions of Common Worship, *and will introduce the following pattern of weekly worship with effect from...*' listing the weekly services, and the rite used.

4 Are we getting all the *Common Worship* liturgy in 2000?

Parts of *Common Worship* have been available since 1998, including the Calendar, Lectionary and Collects, and Initiation Services. The seasonal material, in a book called *Times and Seasons*, and an updated version of *Patterns for Worship* should be published by 2002, in the same format as the *Common Worship* texts. The amended version of the Initiation Services and the Daily Office will also be published later; the weekday lectionary will be published in 2000, but has a short period of authorisation (2000-2004) to allow any weaknesses to be corrected. And the ASB Ordinal has been authorised until 2005, to allow for consultation across the Anglican Communion and ecumenically.

5   What's happening to the *Book of Common Prayer*?

Nothing!   The BCP can only be altered by Act of Parliament. However, the main *Common Worship* volume (see below) does contain some Prayer Book services in their 1928 form, including the Order 2 Holy Communion, Morning and Evening Prayer, Compline, and the Litany. In all, about a quarter of the main volume is in traditional language, and many who use BCP services may prefer the liturgy as it is presented in the *Common Worship* main book.

WHAT SORT OF BOOK ARE WE BEING OFFERED?

6   What will be in the main *Common Worship* book?

Common Worship: Services and Prayers for the Church of England contains all the services and resources which are used regularly on a Sunday in an Anglican parish church. These will include Holy Communion Order 1 (in both modern and traditional language with an ASB structure) and Order 2 (in both traditional and modern language with a BCP structure), and relevant supplementary texts.

There will also be examples of non-eucharistic Sunday services under the heading A Service of the Word. This will include some examples of A Service of the Word; Morning and Evening Prayer on Sunday and Night Prayer (Compline), all in modern and traditional language; other prayers, the Litany; authorised forms of confession and absolution; creeds and authorised affirmations of faith; canticles; and the Church of England version of the ECUSA Psalter. The Coverdale (BCP) Psalter is *not* included in the main book. The updated service of Holy Baptism and the Thanksgiving for the Gift of a Child are included, but the other pastoral offices are published in a separate volume.

The Collects and Post-Communions in modern and traditional language are included, along with the lectionary references, but the Sunday readings are not printed in full. Despite the inclusion of so much traditional language material, the exclusion of weekday material and the Bible readings means that the main book will be about two thirds the size of the ASB. The main book will also be available in large print, and should eventually be published in Braille.

7   **What other *Common Worship* publications are there?**
The main book, published in a plethora of colours and qualities, will be supplemented by

- President's edition (the altar copy), which will include up to two musical settings of each eucharistic prayer

- *Common Worship: Pastoral Services*, which includes Wholeness and Healing, Marriage, and Funeral rites

- Separate booklets for each of the Holy Communion Orders, Morning and Evening Prayer on Sunday, and Night Prayer (Compline) will all be available. There will also be separate booklets for marriages, funerals, baptisms, thanksgivings, and communion for the sick.

The initiation services, currently available in an interim edition, will be republished later as part of *Rites on the Way*.

8 What can we do with our old ASBs?

Some churches will want to continue using their ASBs for the daily office, because the *Common Worship* provision will probably not be authorised until 2001. For those who will not be using their ASBs again after 31 December 2000, please consider recycling them. A legacy of old books in a dusty cupboard for our children to dispose of in twenty years is probably rather unkind!

Some ASBs have been given in memory of a loved one, so pastoral sensitivity will be needed in the process of disposal. You may wish to invite those who donated books to take them back as a memento, and then produce a memorial scroll or plaque to remember the generosity of those who gave ASBs as well as those who have contributed towards *Common Worship*.

9 How long will it be before the services change again?

The *Common Worship* services have been authorised without a time limit, and require a two-thirds majority of General Synod to bring about changes. However, it is certain that new liturgical models and materials will cry out for incorporation into mainstream Anglican worship within the next twenty years, and the process of renewal will begin again. Fortunately, *Common Worship* is published as a series of books rather than one all-encompassing volume, so it should be possible to renew one volume without affecting the others.

HOW WILL IT AFFECT OUR SUNDAY WORSHIP?

10 How is the Communion Service changing?

Those churches that are already using the *Common Worship* Calendar, Lectionary and Collects will know that there is no longer provision for an opening sentence. Instead there is a stronger liturgical opening to the service, in the form of a Trinitarian greeting. Most of the congregational texts of the service are unchanged, or only slightly altered to take account of inclusive language, such as in the Confession. However there are also important changes to the Gospel responses, to the Nicene Creed, and at the beginning of the eucharistic prayer. Both the modified traditional and ASB versions of the Lord's Prayer are printed, and there is an option to use the ecumenical text in the appendix.

Although congregations may feel uneasy when the changes are first introduced, in our experience the new prayers become familiar to a congregation within about two months.

11 What is A Service of the Word?

A Service of the Word is a non-eucharistic service intended as the main act of worship on Sundays or other days. It is a celebration of the Word of God, followed by a congregational response of faith and prayer. In its fullness it also includes opportunities for penitence and praise. Unlike most services, it consists almost entirely of notes, resources and directions, and allows for wide discretion in local use.

12 How do we go about choosing the right texts?

Like many of the Church of England's liturgical publications over the last decade, *Common Worship* gives numerous options for texts that might be used in any service. The notes are an obvious starting point to any individual or group planning a *Common Worship* service, and the services are accompanied by a Service Structure which clearly shows the shape of the liturgy, and a Service Outline that indicates the elements which need to be present. This is especially useful if additional or alternative resources replace parts of the authorised service.

Because of the many options available, expect *Common Worship* services to take more time to plan; many parishes now have a Worship Team of clergy, readers and interested lay people who work together to draft seasonal and special services. The ease and relatively low cost of electronic publishing means that local service books can be reprinted every two or three years, making such collaboration an ongoing part of parish life.

The potential dangers: one clergyman asked if he could make *Common Worship* services look like the ASB! The answer is, basically yes, but what a waste of the potential. And another danger: using a different eucharistic prayer each week, a different confession, a different affirmation of faith ... while this may be liturgically stimulating, it may serve only to confuse, rather than to lead a congregation into worship.

13 Do we have to use the new Collects?

The *Common Worship* Collect of the Day must be used at every parish church Sunday service, unless the service is taken from the BCP. The collects in the ASB cease to be authorised on 31 December 2000, and the new collects are their successors. However, those who are dissatisfied with the *Common Worship* provision may wish to note that from Advent to Candlemas, the collects in *The Promise of His Glory* are still available for use. Some churches have discovered the ICEL scripture-related collects, and are finding them a rich and creative resource for worship, but these are not authorised for use in the Church of England.

14 What music is there to go with the new services?

The Royal School of Church Music (RSCM) is resourcing the music for official publications of *Common Worship*. Each of the eucharistic prayers will have at least one musical setting that will be published in the president's edition of the main book. The RSCM also plans to provide an interim book of musical resources (with a lifespan of 5-7 years), which will include a range of settings in a number of musical styles, for frequently used texts. Settings will be arranged by text rather than by composer, and will include liturgy from the Holy Communion services and the Daily Office, in both modern and traditional language.

Existing music for Holy Communion can generally be used with the small textual amendments to the modern language Nicene Creed, Gospel responses and the third sentence of the opening dialogue in the eucharistic prayer. Churches are not required to use the *Common Worship* Psalter, and can therefore continue to use their own pointed texts.

HOW DO WE MAKE THE CHANGE?

15 What is the first thing to do?

Prepare the congregation for the change to our liturgy. Use parish notice sheets, newsletters and letters to members of the electoral roll (see chapter 8) to communicate about the changeover. Prepare the PCC for the financial implications of *Common Worship*. Finally, plan how the services are best presented in your church. Look at the different options available, and consider using local service books for the first year. This will give the church time to acclimatise to the new liturgy.

16 How do we choose what to buy?

Our advice to churches in Durham Diocese has been to buy only a few copies of the main book initially. Most churches will only need a limited number in any case, and will use either the separate booklets or their own local service books. Church House Publishing will be producing *Common Worship* in electronic editions, as *Visual Liturgy* 3 and as a text disk, and all the authorised texts will also be available free on the Church of England website, to resource the production of local books.

17 How much will this change cost our church?

Church House Publishing are publishing *all* the service books, separate booklets and electronic versions of *Common Worship*. It should be possible to negotiate a discount, particularly on the main book, from local bookshops for bulk purchases. The RRP of the main book is £15, while separate Holy Communion, Marriage and Funeral booklets are £1.65 each. *Visual Liturgy* costs £100 (£35 for the upgrade), but using this it is possible to prepare and copy 100 local service books with card cover and two eucharistic prayers for about £30.

18 Can we produce our own service booklets?

Local service books have a number of advantages

- they are cheaper than the published texts

- local and seasonal variation can be included in the service

- one or two eucharistic prayers can be reproduced in full, improving the appearance of the service.

Visual Liturgy has made the publication of service books very easy. Liturgical texts are presented in full, and all the options are made available, thus lessening the risk of typographical errors; the package makes clear which elements of the service are mandatory; and the format allows fairly easy transfer into a number of different styles of service book and card. Obviously, those with some publishing acumen should be able to manipulate texts without *Visual Liturgy*, but the huge range of resources which accompany the basic services may still make the disk worth purchasing for most parishes.

Copyright must be acknowledged in the form stated at the front of the main book, for example

> Common Worship: Services and Prayers for the Church of England, *material from which is included in this service, is copyright © The Archbishops' Council 2000.*

19 Where can we get more help?

Many Diocesan Liturgical Committees are running training events and publishing local materials to help ease the changeover to *Common Worship*, so it is certainly worth contacting your local DLC first. Diocesan websites can also provide useful information and links. The Durham Liturgical Committee website, for example, is at www.durhamliturgy.freeserve.co.uk

Praxis is an educational organisation sponsored by the Liturgical Commission. They publish a quarterly newsletter and training packs, and run numerous national and local training events. They can be contacted at Sarum College, 19 The Close, Salisbury, SP1 2EE, email praxis@sarum.ac.uk

The Sarum College website at www.sarum.ac.uk also includes details of the Institute for Liturgy and Mission, including material by the Pastoral Musician.

The RSCM is based at Cleveland Lodge, Westhumble, Dorking, RH5 6BW, tel 01306 872800, and they also have a website at www.rscm.com

The Church of England website gives information about *Common Worship* including the full text of all authorised *Common Worship* liturgy. The website is at www.cofe.anglican.org/commonworship, and they can be emailed at common.worship@c-of-e.org.uk

News of Liturgy is published monthly, and can be ordered from Grove Books Ltd, Ridley Hall Road, Cambridge, CB3 9UH, tel 01223 464748.

2
Introducing *Common Worship*

Revising the ASB

For many people – and certainly the tabloid newspapers – the biggest question about *Common Worship* is a simple 'why?'. Why is the Church's liturgy changing again, why is it changing *now*, and why is it changing all at once? The ASB has been a regular and much-valued part of the Church's life for so long that we forget that it was originally intended to last just ten years. In fact it has served the Church for twice that long, and over the course of the last two decades its services and prayers have entered the lifeblood of the Church at a profound level. Indeed, the Rite A eucharist may be all that a great many worshippers have ever known or can easily remember. It would probably come as quite a shock to most people to discover that services in modern English were almost unheard of only thirty years ago, and that communion services in the familiar ASB 'shape' were introduced into the Church of England as recently as 1967.

A century of liturgical change

The ASB is itself the product of much liturgical *angst* and reform. For many decades the process of change was anything but straightforward, mostly because of the Church of England's unique relationship with the secular powers. Until the 1960s, the power to change the Church's liturgy lay with Parliament, and the only services officially permitted were those in the 1662 *Book of Common Prayer*. As long ago as 1906, a Royal Commission had reported that the Prayer Book services were 'too narrow for the religious life of the present generation', and the Church embarked on a long project of reform. When the new Prayer Book – a somewhat modest revision of the old – was finally presented to Parliament for approval in 1927 and 1928, the House of Commons twice refused to authorise it. With the bishops' blessing, many parts of the book came into general use nevertheless; and although this was a clear challenge to the authority of Parliament and the settlement between Church and State, the point was not pressed.

Following a great deal of discussion and debate, the control of Parliament over the Church's worship was loosened considerably in 1966 and effectively disappeared altogether in 1973. Parliament retained its control over the 1662 Prayer Book, but the General Synod is free to authorise any further services or prayer books that it wishes to, and to discontinue their use as appropriate.

The first new services authorised in the 1960s were Series 1, a set of lightly revised 1928 services, and Series 2, more radical revisions of Prayer Book services, though still using 'thee/thou/thine' language. In the 1970s, a full set of services in contemporary language was released (Series 3). These were collected together and published, with small amendments, as the ASB in 1980. The ASB also contains a traditional-language eucharistic rite (Rite B, a revision of Series 1 and Series 2) and the 1977 Joint Liturgical Group (JLG) lectionary, with its two-year thematic cycle of readings.

Why are we revising the ASB *now*?

Quite simply, because its authorisation period ends in December 2000; and while it has been an immensely successful resource, there are many areas in which it now needs further revision.

- *Inclusive language*
  For good or ill, the sensitivity to language is here to stay: it is not possible to speak today of men, mankind, and fellow men with the same innocence as we did 20 years ago.

- *Richness of idiom*
  Like any written work, the ASB is a child of its time, and the liturgical writing of the 1960s and 1970s is now widely regarded as concise and rather flat. Since then a richer, more poetic approach to liturgical writing has been apparent, for example in *Lent, Holy Week, Easter* (1986) and particularly in *The Promise of His Glory* (1991).

- *The need for greater flexibility*
  Few would now defend the lack of variety in the four eucharistic prayers in Rite A, or the canticles in the daily office. The increasing use of supplementary books (*Patterns for Worship* and *Enriching the Christian Year*) and seasonal material (*Lent, Holy Week, Easter* and *The Promise of His Glory*) has increased the appetite for more variety around a common core.

- *Fresh thinking on initiation and other services*
  The publication of the report *On the Way* marked a new approach to baptism and confirmation, in which initiation rites are regarded as steps along a journey of faith rather than complete acts in themselves. This changing approach demands a different liturgical expression. The influence of ecumenical dialogue and fresh study is also apparent in the approach to other services, such as the funeral rite and the daily office.

What kind of book?

There was a lively debate through the 1970s as to how the new services should be made available. What emerged then was a complete 'all-in-one' alternative prayer book – the 1300-page ASB.

This time there is a core book containing the services used on Sundays, in both Prayer Book and *Common Worship* forms. Other books containing the pastoral offices and seasonal material will supplement the main book.

However, it is doubtful whether all parishes will need to buy many copies of the new book. The text of all services will be available electronically, and many parishes are already used to producing their own service booklets with *Visual Liturgy*, often in several versions, varying with the seasons.

All this has profound implications for our concept of *common prayer*. We moved thirty years ago from all using one Prayer Book (albeit flexibly) to using a multiplicity of rites; now each parish is able to produce its own local versions of those rites. The ideal of common prayer is no longer about using the same Prayer Book, or even about using one of a limited range of services; it has far more to do with ethos, style, and a recognisable structure centred around a common core of texts. This change in attitude has already entered the life of the Church with the use of seasonal resources and particularly *Patterns for Worship*, and will continue with *Common Worship*.

The ethos of *Common Worship*

The last 20 years have seen a fresh creativity in liturgical writing, giving the Church a richer and more varied approach to worship. At the same time, there is a strong consensus that we need a common core of well-known texts, both to preserve our sense of unity as Anglicans and to celebrate the historical continuity of our worship with the BCP and the liturgical tradition of the wider church. The creative tension between these two developments defines the context in which the *Common Worship* service were written, and the structure and language of the new rites reflect both the memory of our Christian heritage and the diverse culture within which the Gospel is proclaimed, celebrated and lived today.

Since the ASB was introduced in 1980, a number of official and semi-official publications have reflected on the nature of worship and its relationship to our journey of faith, the spiritual needs of individuals and congregations, and the society in which the Church must live and minister. The main points of this developing thinking include

- *Evolving core*
  Liturgy is formed and celebrated within a culture; and our culture, both inside and outside the church, is changing rapidly. The liturgy must therefore reflect our unity and identity as Anglicans: it must give a family likeness to our worship, while allowing for variety and diversity around a liturgical and doctrinal core. Both for the spiritual comfort of the individual, and for the integration of the local church within the wider church, it is vital that this liturgical core resonates with a sense of belonging.

- *Unity and variety*
  The new rites reflect this pattern of a strong common core surrounded by variety and flexibility. In the baptism rite, for instance, the service is built around Preparation, the Liturgy of the Word, the Liturgy of

Baptism, the Prayers, the Liturgy of the Eucharist, and the Sending Out. Additional material – the variety around this common core – is added in appendices, including seasonal material with a wide diversity of presidential and congregational texts.

- *Journey*

  The sense that all life is a pilgrimage and a journey is deeply rooted in the Jewish and Christian traditions. It is strongly celebrated in the services in the BCP, and, in a slightly different form, in the ASB. *Common Worship* continues this tradition and seeks to tease it out still further. The new calendar strengthens the idea of a liturgical journey from Incarnation to Cross and Resurrection. In the same way, the new eucharistic texts reflect the Christian life as a journey of discipleship and growth, along which we all travel. This theme is seen at its strongest in the initiation rites, where the journey of the individual and of the whole Church is emphasised and explored. The pastoral rites surrounding marriage and death similarly mark important transitions in our pilgrimage, and the new services draw this out very clearly.

- *Cultural changes*

  In our post-modern culture, with a pick-and-mix society increasingly influencing the Church, there is a significant demand for flexibility in worship. Where Iona worship and Greek Orthodoxy meet and rub shoulders liturgically, there needs to be sufficient flexibility in the core texts to contain such pressures.

- *Integration of mission, learning, spirituality and liturgy*

  Bishop John Gladwin writes: 'Some [liturgies] ... can impart the challenge and the welcome of the Gospel without undermining the integrity of those who do not call themselves Christians' (*The Renewal of Common Prayer*, p. 42). In *Common Worship* we find a liturgy designed not only to sustain and nurture the faithful, but also to provide for those whose heritage is Anglican, yet who rarely attend church services. There is also a missionary edge to the new rites, to encourage the Church to proclaim the Gospel in lives dedicated to God's praise and glory.

Practical considerations

- *Cleaning up the page*

  Many rubrics have effectively been removed from the body of the text and placed with the introductory notes. This puts more responsibility on those leading services, to ensure that they have a basic understanding of the liturgy; it also means that the text of services is generally easier to follow. For the same reason, many variant texts, which were printed in the main body of the service in the ASB, have been moved to appendices in *Common Worship*. This, of course, carries the danger that the text as printed will become normative, and supplementary material will simply be ignored. These problems can be overcome by the use of local service books.

- *Tightening up the structure, loosening up the text*

  The same 'clean page' approach is also apparent in a tightening of the structure of the new services. In the Order 1 eucharist, for example, the prayers of penitence are printed only once, at the beginning of the service, and not in two places as in the ASB. A note allows them to be used at the later position, but the normal expectation is that they will be used as part of the Preparation.

At the same time, there is encouragement to greater flexibility in terms of the texts themselves. For example, where Rite A suggests three alternative forms of intercession, Order 1 offers five. Even more significantly, Order 1 actively encourages a diversity of use by printing only an outline structure for the prayers in the main body of the text.

- *'Eucharistic' structure to the pastoral rites*
  Unlike their ASB predecessors, the *Common Worship* baptism, marriage and funeral rites all incorporate a strong and coherent Liturgy of the Word modelled closely on the first part of the eucharist. This gives them a much more satisfactory structure when used as stand-alone services in their own right, and it also makes the integration of the rites within the eucharist much more satisfactory than before.

'Owning' *Common Worship*

Any change in worship creates a sense of crisis for some, and of unbounded enthusiasm for others! Most of us feel a mixture of these emotions. Not least among the anxieties felt by many parishes will be the potential cost of yet another set of service books, or the burden of having to produce a new range of local booklets.

But as the teething problems are overcome, it is to be hoped that the evocative poetry of the *Common Worship* services, and their ethos of journey and story, will commend the new rites not only to clergy and to those leading worship, but also to congregations who are touched both by the richness and the deep historic stability of the new material.

3
Holy Communion

The eucharist in *Common Worship* may at first appear confusing, because whereas the ASB had just two rites, *Common Worship* has four. In fact things are considerably clearer with the new services. There are two basic orders, and their distinction is not in their language, but in their shape. Order 1 follows the pattern of the primitive Christian eucharist, widely used ecumenically, and familiar in the Church of England since 1967. Order 2 follows the pattern of the Communion Service in the BCP. Both orders come in a contemporary language and a traditional language form, and the four variants are printed in full for the sake of greater clarity and ease of use. By contrast, the ASB provision was rather less clear, because beneath the apparent simplicity of Rites A and B lurked many different ways of celebrating each service.

Order 1

During the liturgical revisions of the 1960s and 1970s, far more time was spent working on the eucharist than on any other service, and the work put in then has proved remarkably enduring. Nevertheless, twenty years' frequent use of Rite A has exposed certain weaknesses in structure and language. Order 1 is recognisably a direct successor to Rite A, and clearly builds upon its strengths; but there are also some worthwhile improvements, providing greater clarity, simplicity, variety and devotional balance.

The ethos of Order 1

The first priority was to give the eucharist a *clearer shape*, so that the printed text is both 'cleaner' in appearance, and also has a tighter structure. As a result, Order 1 has far less material printed in the main text. For example the confession is printed just once, at the beginning of the rite, rather than being also printed in the middle (though a rubric allows its use at the later position when appropriate). And many of the variable texts – those for the intercessions, the introduction to the peace, the preparation of the table, and all eight eucharistic prayers – are printed in appendices rather than in the main body of the service.

While the deep structure of the rite is therefore made clearer in Order 1, there is at the same time a 'loosening up' of the service in places where the shape is not at issue: what Kenneth Stevenson has called the *soft points* of the liturgy (*Liturgy for a New Century*, pp. 29-43). There is consequently a much wider selection of variable, seasonal texts for use at the intercession, the peace, the preparation of the table and so on. This encourages the use of seasonal prayers, and of freer forms of prayer generally, by refusing to 'canonise' one particular form for general use. We might note that the post-communion prayers published in 1997 with *Calendar, Lectionary and Collects* are a further step in the same direction.

It may seem that these two trends – greater simplicity on the one hand, and greater variety on the other – are pulling in opposite directions, but it is more useful to see them as complementing each other. The basic shape of the rite needs clear and consistent expression, and core texts – particularly prayers said together by the whole congregation – need to be familiar and fixed. But other prayers and introductions, especially those spoken by the ministers, can exhibit a rich variety without in the least compromising the clarity of the service.

The main changes from Rite A

- Order 1 has a much stronger and more coherent beginning to the service. Opening sentences have gone: instead, the traditional invocation of the Holy Trinity may be used. Any informal introduction, welcome and notices are given *after* the liturgical greeting.

- A more formal greeting may be used as an alternative to 'The Lord be with you'

  Grace, mercy and peace from God our Father
  and the Lord Jesus Christ be with you
  and also with you.

- Two forms of confession are printed in the text: the familiar ASB form, altered for inclusive language, and an alternative, which avoids the (slightly controversial) confession of sin against other people. Suitable penitential kyries may be used instead of either.

- Silence is enjoined before the collect, thus restoring its original intention as a prayer which gathers up the silent prayers of the congregation, prior to the Liturgy of the Word.

- Gospel acclamations ('Alleluias') may be said or sung before the Gospel, instead of a hymn. Seasonal forms are provided, as well as a selection for ordinary time. For example, in Advent

> *Alleluia, alleluia.*
> *Prepare the way of the Lord,*
> *make his paths straight,*
> *and all flesh shall see the salvation of God.*
> **Alleluia.**

and in ordinary time

> *Alleluia, alleluia.*
> *I am the light of the world, says the Lord.*
> *Whoever follows me will never walk in darkness*
> *but will have the light of life.*
> **Alleluia.**

• The gospel responses are addressed directly to Christ. These are simply a modern translation of the Rite B text

> *Hear the Gospel of our Lord Jesus Christ*
> *according to N.*
> **Glory to you, O Lord.**

> *This is the Gospel of the Lord.*
> **Praise to you, O Christ.**

• The offertory prayers are clearly marked as optional, and a much greater variety is provided. One example is a reworking of an early Christian text (from the *Didache*) with a distinctive eschatological echo

> *As the grain once scattered in the fields*
> *and the grapes once dispersed on the hillside*
> *are now reunited on this table in bread and wine,*
> *so, Lord, may your whole Church*
> *soon be gathered together*
> *from the corners of the earth into your kingdom.*
> **Amen.**

- At the breaking of the bread, an alternative text is provided

    Every time we eat this bread and drink this cup,
    we proclaim the Lord's death until he comes

    or the breaking can be done during *Agnus Dei.*

- Post-communion prayers replace the ASB post-communion sentences.

Ministries

Liturgy is far more than the text on the page – it is an act of worship, and the *way* it is celebrated matters quite as much as *what* is said. The notes and rubrics are therefore an important element of the liturgical resource.

The notes contain a very substantial comment on ministries. First, the ministry of the *whole people of God* is affirmed, both in their active participation throughout the service, and in specific ministry by certain individuals, such as those reading lessons or leading intercessions.

The *president* holds the whole service together from beginning to end. He or she greets the congregation, says the absolution, prays the collect, introduces the peace, says the eucharistic prayer, breaks the bread, and pronounces the blessing. The bishop, when present, would usually preside.

Where there is an assistant minister (whether another priest, a deacon, a Reader or other authorised layperson) the notes strongly suggest that he or she should take the traditional *deacon's role.* In its fullness this role includes introducing and leading the prayers of penitence, proclaiming the gospel, leading the intercessions, preparing the table, assisting in the administration of communion, the ablutions, and the dismissal. The liturgical deacon may also lead the congregational acclamations in the eucharistic prayer (see below).

While other patterns of shared ministry are also possible, we hope that this priest/deacon arrangement will be given a fair try, especially in traditions where it may not have been explored before. It has the potential to express a genuinely shared ministry far more satisfactorily than (say) a Reader leading the Ministry of the Word and the priest 'taking over' at the offertory. While this way of working admittedly takes more preparation and care in order to do it well, it also has the advantage of encouraging more sensitive liturgical leadership.

Eucharistic prayers

The eucharistic prayer is rich in imagery, symbolism, drama and language. It proclaims and celebrates what the Christian community is, and who God is, and how he acts among us.

It is always a *responsive* prayer, with a part for the presiding priest and a part for the congregation (and sometimes a part for an assisting minister too). It is a *dramatic* prayer, in which a story is told and our faith is proclaimed and celebrated. That dramatic celebration can take on a variety of different forms, depending on the mood of the service. And it is a *purposeful* prayer, in which something is accomplished.

Order 1 contains eight eucharistic prayers. The first three are revisions of ASB prayers, while the other five are new to the Church of England. The new prayers employ much more vibrant imagery and richer language than hitherto.

Significantly, they all have a *single* invocation of the Holy Spirit, avoiding the 'double epiclesis' of the ASB prayers (one invocation over the elements before the words of institution, and another on the worshippers afterwards). In four of the new prayers (D, F, G, and H) the epiclesis comes in the traditional eastern position, *after* the words of institution.

Opportunity is given for substantial congregational involvement in four of the prayers. Prayer D has a set of acclamations running through the prayer, and acclamations may optionally be used in prayers A and F as well. It is not necessary for the president to lead these: the role falls naturally to the liturgical deacon. Prayer H has an even greater degree of participation, with substantial responses for the congregation which do not merely echo the words of the president, but move the prayer forward.

A full set of short seasonal prefaces is provided for prayers A, B, and C; and for the first time, extended prefaces are also provided, intended to replace all the text between the opening dialogue and the Sanctus. These may be used with prayers A, B and E. (There is no provision for seasonal material in prayers D, F, G, and H.)

Prayer A is a conflation of ASB Prayers 1 and 2, lightly revised. As in ASB 2, the majority of the preface may be replaced with a seasonal paragraph. The anamnesis ('we make the memorial') derives from ASB 2, and the familiar 'renew us by your Spirit, inspire us with your love ...' and the responsive doxology are retained from ASB 1.

Prayer B is a light revision of ASB 3, a prayer along the lines of the early Christian prayer of Hippolytus.

Prayer C   adheres closely to ASB 4, offering a eucharistic prayer which follows the cadences of the Prayer Book consecration.

Prayer D   is a responsive prayer, intended particularly for occasions when children are present. It is simple in structure and language, but vivid in its imagery.

Prayer E   is the only new prayer to retain the classical western shape. Its concise 'normal' preface will seem thin in comparison with the richness of the rest of the prayer; Prayer E is clearly best used with an extended preface.

Prayer F   is consciously modelled along eastern lines. It ends with a short series of intercessions for the church and the world. This is a rich and joyful prayer, to be celebrated at a solemn pace.

Prayer G   employs vivid paradox (e.g. 'silent music') and a distinctive oblation: 'we plead with confidence his sacrifice ...'. Again there is intercession, with the option of extempore prayer.

Prayer H   represents a conscious attempt to involve the congregation not only in acclamations of praise, but also in contributing to the momentum of the eucharistic action. The ending is worthy of note: the desire to write a eucharistic prayer culminating in the Sanctus has been around for some forty years, but has only now been realised in this prayer.

Order 1 in Traditional Language

This version of Order 1 will be seen as the natural successor to ASB Rite B, but offers more freedom. With very few exceptions, there is the same liberty to use seasonal or other texts as in Order 1. The two services are identical in structure and very close in wording. For example, the traditional language post-communion prayer and dismissal sentence have been conformed to the Rite A / Order 1 form.

Two eucharistic prayers are provided – traditional language versions of prayers A and C. They both have memorial acclamations.

Curiously, both forms of the Lord's Prayer are printed, despite the unlikelihood of a church opting for a traditional language service wishing to pray this prayer in contemporary language.

Order 1 in Traditional Language will satisfy most people who used Rite B, and will particularly please those who were frustrated with its lack of flexibility.

Order 2

Parishes using the Prayer Book Communion Service with alterations were not well served by the ASB. Few churches would wish to use the Ten Commandments, the Collect for the Monarch, and one of the Exhortations at every celebration. At the same time, many parishes add an Old Testament reading, a psalm, Gospel responses, a wider selection of proper prefaces, and the Agnus Dei. Finally, in some parishes it is customary to rearrange some of the material in order to unite the Eucharistic Preface, the Prayer of Consecration and the Prayer of Oblation in one prayer.

Order 2 provides for this need. As printed, it is a fairly conservative version of 'The Prayer Book as used', which will be widely welcomed. Those requiring more radical variations will probably need to print their own service books, taking advantage of the permission in the notes to rearrange the elements of the eucharistic prayer.

Just as Order 1 has a traditional language variant, Order 2 also has a modern language variant, intended for those who wish to worship in contemporary language while retaining the doctrinal emphases of the Prayer Book service. However, in contrast with the close conformity of structure and text between the two forms of Order 1, there are more freedoms and alternatives in the contemporary form of Order 2. Most useful of all will be the free choice of intercessions as in Order 1, and many will also welcome the alternative confession and the inclusion of the prayer 'Merciful God' as an alternative prayer of humble access.

4

A Service of the Word

Although the balance has changed with time, Anglican worship has always consisted of a mixture of sacramental and non-sacramental services. At the beginning of this century, Matins was the main Sunday service in most parishes; today, the eucharist has largely supplanted it. Alongside these regular Sunday services there has always been a need for something else – a form of non-eucharistic worship more flexible and responsive than Morning or Evening Prayer. Until very recently, there was no official provision, and therefore no help, for putting together family services, preaching services and the like. A Service of the Word is designed to meet this need. The new service was authorised in 1993, and is printed in full in *Patterns for Worship* (1995) along with a substantial body of resource material. Because some of the resources have been slightly modified in *Common Worship*, a new form of *Patterns for Worship* is to be re-published within the next 2 years, alongside the revised book of seasonal material, *Times and Seasons*.

The main book, *Common Worship: Services and Prayers for the Church of England,* will include sample services and resources for A Service of the Word, and Morning and Evening Prayer on Sunday and Night Prayer, in both modern and traditional language.

A service without texts

For those used to Anglican service books, the most startling thing about A Service of the Word is that there are no texts! Nowhere is the minister told what to say, or the congregation how to respond. Instead there is an outline order of service and a set of instructions. A Service of the Word is not intended to be prescriptive, but rather to help those planning and leading worship to ensure that services contain all the essential ingredients, held together in a satisfactory balance and with a good sense of liturgical flow. Much has been made of the fact that Christian life is a pilgrimage or 'journey', and liturgy reflects this in a variety of ways, not least in the way each service needs its own clear sense of 'journey' as it proceeds. A number of important landmarks have to be visited in a coherent order, with each given its due weight.

The service begins with the gathering of the congregation as the people of God. The congregation acknowledges God, and itself as the redeemed people of God, in penitence and worship; and gathers up its prayers in the Collect.

The Ministry of the Word is the heart of the service, in which the Word of God – the story of God's work and grace in the midst of his people – is read, celebrated and preached.

The congregation responds to God in prayer, praise and faith. A creed or other affirmation of faith concludes the Ministry of the Word. Payers of intercession, thanksgivings and the Lord's Prayer follow.

Finally, the service is brought to a conclusion in prayer or blessing, and the congregation is sent out in Christ's name.

Planning A Service of the Word

A Service of the Word needs a clear *focus*. At the eucharist, the focus is on the sacramental celebration: remembrance, thanksgiving, and the receiving of communion. At A Service of the Word, the focus is – or should be – on the celebration of God's Word, as it is read, preached and responded to in prayer. This is an important point, especially when A Service of the Word is being used as an alternative to the eucharist. It would be misguided, for example, to try to construct a pseudo-eucharistic rite, with the eucharistic prayer and communion replaced by the General Thanksgiving; that would undermine the centrality of the scriptures and the prayers.

Common Worship: Services and Prayers for the Church of England will, like *Patterns,* provide a number of sample services. Any one of these can be used as it stands, but it may be better to take their title seriously, see them as samples, seek to understand how they are put together, and then give some thought to exactly what would work in the local context.

The ethos behind A Service of the Word is that worship should be planned and 'owned' by more than just the priest, and that it should be used flexibly to reflect the season, context, and local custom. Ideally, services should be put together by a worship team, and should not be fixed too rigidly. Many parishes will want to print their own orders of service. Certainly the congregation need some texts in their hands if they are to participate in the core texts such as the prayers of penitence and the creed. A parish could either produce a number of service forms for the different seasons of the year, or a single card with a number of familiar texts printed on it, leaving freedom to vary ministerial texts as appropriate.

The starting point should always be the service outline. Firstly, ask what the service is seeking to achieve. For example, an informal family service, with children present throughout, demands quite a different approach from an evening, mostly adult, service of prayer and meditation. Another challenge is to devise A Service of the Word for use instead of the eucharist when a priest is unavailable. How many texts from the eucharist should be retained? What is the right balance between distinctiveness and familiarity? Whatever the occasion, a clear sense of purpose goes a long way towards determining the shape and content of the service.

Choosing texts

Texts of central importance like the prayers of penitence and the creed must be chosen from among authorised material. Other texts can be chosen more freely, but even here a rich provision of resource material is available, which can be used as it stands or easily adapted. Much of this material can also be used at the eucharist

- *Introductions*
  Greetings and other responsive ways of gathering the congregation and beginning the service

- *Penitential material*
  Invitations to confession, forms of confession, penitential kyries, and forms of absolution

- *Affirmations of Faith*
  Responsive forms of the historic creeds and scriptural affirmations of faith

- *Prayers*
  Litanies and responsive prayers; concluding prayers and post-communion prayers

- *Praise*
  Canticles; acclamations and responsories; proper prefaces for the eucharist

- *Peace*
  Introductory words at the peace

- *Blessings and endings*
  Concluding prayers; solemn (three-fold) blessings; seasonal blessings.

Filling in the details

- *Liturgical beginnings and endings*
  The service requires a strong beginning and ending. This is more than simply a matter of the words used. The way they are said; the place in which the minister stands; a short pause before the greeting or dismissal is spoken – all these will contribute to the congregation's sense of clarity in being called to worship, and being sent out for Christian life and service.

- *Readings*
  On Sunday mornings, the Principal Service readings from the *Calendar, Lectionary and Collects* would normally be used. At A Service of the Word in the evening, where there has already been a morning eucharist or Matins, the Second Service readings would probably be more appropriate.

- *Shared leadership*

  It should be clear who is leading. When someone other than a priest leads the service, 'us' and 'our' are said in the absolution instead of 'you' and 'your', and the ending of the service does not include a blessing.

- *Sermon slot*

  The term sermon may include less formal exposition, the use of drama, interviews, discussion and audio-visuals. This gives tremendous scope to preachers to explore new ways of expressing and interpreting the Word of God.

- *Who may preach?*

  A Service of the Word may be prepared and led by a group of lay people, none of whom is licensed to preach. The Church's rules require that one sermon be preached in every Parish Church each Sunday. If a sermon is being preached at some other service on the same day by a licensed preacher, then, in principle, no problem should arise with someone else giving a suitable meditation or address, or co-ordinating a dramatic presentation, etc, at A Service of the Word. It should be done with the support of the Church Council and at the priest's invitation.

Morning and Evening Prayer on Sunday

Because Morning and Evening Prayer can be celebrated in a variety of ways – everything from a simple form of prayer at the beginning and ending of the day to the Principal Sunday Service – these forms of prayer are considerably more flexible than those in the ASB. The central core of the Ministry of the Word is supplemented by a wide variety of Canticles, and Prayers of Thanksgiving (for the Word, for

Holy Baptism, for the Healing Ministry of the Church, and for the Mission of the Church). Those churches that have experience of using *Celebrating Common Prayer* (CCP) will see clear echoes of it in *Common Worship*.

The service starts with the Preparation, and the Prayers of Penitence. Because Morning and Evening Prayer are *Services of the Word,* seasonal variations can be made, and indeed are encouraged. Where available, the texts for canticles are taken from ELLC, with minimal changes: these include the Benedictus, the Te Deum, the Magnificat and the Nunc Dimittis. The Psalter is a reworking of the American (ECUSA) Psalter, and it includes the modifications already introduced in CCP. It will not be fully pointed, but since its use is not mandatory, those churches which have a custom of singing the psalms are free to continue using their current versions. It is expected that the prayers of intercession which follow the Ministry of the Word should not be narrow in their focus, but broadly based, and that they should form a significant element in the service. Finally, the liturgical ending of the service is strengthened.

Morning and Evening Prayer in traditional language are from the BCP, with permitted variations. This allows the services to be used in their 1928 form, which is the most common variation to the 1662 offices.

Night Prayer (Compline)

Two orders for Compline are provided. The contemporary language Order for Night Prayer will be very familiar to users of the CCP Office. The Order for Night Prayer in Traditional Language is based on the 1928 form (omitting the Creed), with some modest CCP influence.

5
Initiation Services

The guiding principles behind the new initiation services are found in the Synod Report *On the Way: Towards an Integrated Approach to Christian Initiation* (1995). Coming to faith is essentially seen as a journey, embracing growth in belief, prayer and worship, and an appropriate way of life. It is hoped that churches will form a coherent strategy for the evangelism, initiation and growth of new adult believers, and for the care and nurture of those brought to baptism in infancy.

The *Common Worship* Initiation Services were first published in 1998, and in due course will be republished as part of *Rites on the Way* with corrections and some changes (see below). The collection includes orders for Holy Baptism, Confirmation, the Affirmation of Baptismal Faith, and Reception into the Communion of the Church of England. Holy Baptism is also included in the main book.

HOLY BAPTISM

Baptism is the formal starting place in a journey of discipleship, and the *Common Worship* baptism service has a more significant position in the liturgical life of the church than the ASB service. This rite cannot easily be 'scrunched into a 10 minute box' within a Sunday service. The liturgy for baptism is designed to permeate the whole service, from the opening greeting to the presentation of the candle at the end, and the role of the congregation in welcoming and upholding the candidates in their new life in Christ is emphasised.

The *Common Worship* orders for Holy Baptism make provision for the baptism of both adults and children. Four rites are included: Holy Baptism, Baptism outside the eucharist, Baptism of children at the eucharist, and Baptism of children at A Service of the Word. Where young children are baptised, two questions of intent are asked of the parents and godparents at the presentation, who then make the baptismal decision in the name of the *child* (and not also for themselves, as in ASB). The duties of parents and godparents form part of the Commission, which in *Common Worship* comes after baptism.

The importance of signs and symbols is stressed. For example, at the signing with the cross, which follows the Decision, the signing may be made with oil, and sponsors, parents, and godparents may also make the sign of the cross on the forehead of the candidates. At the conclusion of the service, the Sending Out, a lighted candle may be given as a sign of the candidates' ongoing participation in Christ's mission. Appendices include seasonal material drawing on biblical baptismal imagery appropriate to the season, for Epiphany/Baptism of Christ/Trinity, for Easter/Pentecost, and for All Saints.

The recent changes to *Common Worship* Baptism

Unfortunately, there have been significant teething troubles with the 1998 text of the *Common Worship* baptism service. This is partly because some churches are finding that their previous practice at baptism does not work as well with the new liturgy. However, many of the problems have arisen because of the sheer wordiness of the services. Because of these difficulties, General Synod has authorised Rules to Order the Service, which amend the Initiation Service as published in 1998. Texts previously mandatory have become optional, and this should significantly ease the pressure on service length. It may not be appropriate to instigate all the options – churches may choose to keep the intercessions, for instance, but drop some of the readings.

The new rules to order the service include the following alterations to the 1998 Initiation Services book

- The printed introduction becomes optional

- The Gospel reading may be used alone, or with one or two other readings from the lectionary

- The presentation of the candidates is optional

- The ASB three-fold decision is to be included in an appendix, as an alternative to the *Common Worship* six-fold decision, for use when there are good pastoral reasons

- The newly baptised who are able to answer for themselves do not now have to answer the questions following the commission

- The commission may be omitted when its contents are included in the sermon

- Intercessions are optional

- The current ending can usefully be altered to a more acceptable pattern of post communion prayers, (hymn), candle, blessing, dismissal.

Good practice in baptism services

- *Enacting the journey*
  Churches are using the drama of the liturgy to move around the church building, with processions to the font, placing the baptism party on the chancel steps facing the congregation and priest for the decisions, and so on.

- *Making the most of the symbolism*
  of water, oil and the candle – the water can be poured (preferably from a height) throughout the prayer over the water; those sharing in the leading of the service and, if appropriate, parents, godparents, grandparents, or siblings could share in the signing with oil.

- *Sharing liturgical ministry*
  The baptismal candle, lit from the altar or paschal candle, can be given by a member of the congregation, possibly a sponsor who has got to know the family through baptism preparation.

- *Make the most of the calendar*
  Seasonal material for the Epiphany and the Baptism of Christ, for Easter, and for All Saints' tide can be used to good effect throughout the year.

- *Including the whole family*
  For some churches, the exploration of the place of initiation has gone hand in hand with the place of children in our worship, and receiving children to communion.

- *The paschal candle*
  is perhaps better lit before the service starts, rather than at the decision, reflecting continuity with Easter.

- *Word limitation*
  dropping some of the optional texts does help to keep the service to an hour. Some churches are also combining part of the commission with the sermon when appropriate.

Baptism as a 'stand alone' service

- The service assumes a corporate church context for the baptism – it may be that the question to the congregation is omitted in a Sunday afternoon service, or that representative members of the congregation are present to answer on behalf of the wider church.

- The short ministry of the word may be used more comfortably following the commission (and peace) than near the beginning of the service.

- Using music, even recorded music, greatly enhances the 'feel' of the service.

- Families, godparents and sponsors could be encouraged to attend the main Sunday service on a preceding Sunday for the signing with the cross, or on a subsequent Sunday to receive the welcome and candle.

Baptism at the main Sunday service

- A Service of the Word may be a more inclusive context than a communion service for families who do not normally attend church.

- Action, movement, symbolism, and music are all-important considerations, especially at a service where more children than normal are usually present.

Providing colouring materials and books is often sensible too!

- Consider involving members of the baptism team or others in the service itself, perhaps as sponsors, in leading intercessions, or in giving the candle.

THE OTHER INITIATION SERVICES

Common Worship also includes orders for

- Confirmation of those baptised as children

- Affirmation of Baptismal Faith – for those who have come to a lively faith following a period away from the Church, or who wish to renew their faith but have been previously baptised and confirmed

- Reception into the Church of England – for those becoming Anglicans from other Christian communions who have already been episcopally confirmed.

Confirmation

Candidates may give a personal testimony after the presentation, or may ask a sponsor to speak for them. When a large number of candidates are being confirmed, time may preclude this, but the service book could include a paragraph of testimony, or a suitable drawing or poem from each person being confirmed.

The profession of faith takes place at the font if possible, to recall baptism, and may be followed by sprinkling with water or signing with oil. The commission from the baptism rite may be used after confirmation, particularly when the service includes baptism as well as confirmation.

Many dioceses have a pack of material which provides resources for confirmation services. These may include particularly suitable hymns and prayers, and examples of previous services, which indicate the bishop's preference for using oil, or for using the font for the profession of faith, and so on.

THANKSGIVING FOR THE GIFT OF A CHILD

Thanksgiving for the Gift of a Child is one of a series of *Rites on the Way,* which were crafted by the late Michael Vasey as a resource to surround the whole process of initiation and growth in the Christian faith. These rites are intended as a resource for the spiritual journey of an individual within the wider church community.

Unfortunately, with Michael's death in 1998, this work has been put on hold, and the bulk of *Rites on the Way* is not being published with the other *Common Worship* liturgy. One exception is the service of Thanksgiving for the Gift of a Child, which can perhaps be seen as Michael's bequest to the Church of England.

The rite may be used in a number of settings, from a private thanksgiving at home or in church, with only family and close friends present, to a public celebration of the adoption or birth of a number of children as part of the main Sunday service. For some people it will be seen as a preliminary to baptism, and as such could be used when families first approach a local church requesting baptism, and before a period of preparation. Those families who do not want to have their child baptised, but who do want to acknowledge God and give thanks to God for their child, may find it useful.

In order to emphasise that a service of thanksgiving is not a baptism, it is suggested that a register be kept of those for whom this service has been conducted, and a certificate given.

6
Pastoral Services

The Pastoral Services are not printed in the main service book, but in a separate volume. They consist of services of Wholeness and Healing, the Marriage Service and the Funeral rites, which are all concerned with a particular sequence of stages in our Christian journey. These stages call for a careful blend of corporate celebration and individual prayer and reflection; the *Common Worship* provision is generous with both, offering a core service with a wealth of resource material for pastoral ministry before and after a marriage, death or prayer for healing.

Each service is provided with a Pastoral Introduction, which is designed to be printed at the front of a service card or book, to be read privately by worshippers before the service. These texts acknowledge the reason for the gathering, the pastoral implications of sharing together in a Christian journey, and in joining our individual stories with the story of the wider church through the ages. In each case they encourage the individual to participate in the life of the people of God, and to look for the active incarnation of God in their own lives.

A spoken Preface or Introduction follows the Liturgical Greeting and the Welcome at the start of the service. These texts also give voice to the reason for the gathering, and to the process or journey of the liturgy which will lead the congregation towards God.

The notes are an obvious starting point to an individual or team planning services, and the accompanying Service

Structure is intended to show the shape of the liturgy. The Service Outline gives a strong indication of the elements which need to be present if additional or alternative liturgy replaces parts of the authorised service.

WHOLENESS AND HEALING

The theology of the rite

Wholeness and Healing is set within the context of Christian initiation, since all forms of reconciliation and healing are further stages along the Christian journey begun in baptism, leading ultimately to fullness of life in Christ. Central to this collection of rites are a number of *corporate* rather than *private* liturgies, relating the individual perspective strongly to the activity of the whole Church. Thus the theology of belonging to the faith by baptism, and the proclamation of salvation by the whole Church, is united within the Church's public worship, from which more individual and private ministry may then come.

Wholeness and Healing in *Common Worship* incorporates most of *Ministry to the Sick* (1983, a supplement to the ASB), either in the main text or commended material. However, considerable additional material is also made available to the Church of England, with the hope that the services will be more accessible to those unused to regular church attendance, as well as showing greater sensitivity to ecumenical concerns. The Liturgical Commission has kept the language simple, the imagery direct and the rites brief.

What's in Wholeness and Healing?

- The theology of the Rites, and an Introductory Note

- Celebration of Wholeness and Healing – a service especially suitable for a diocesan or a deanery occasion

- Laying on of Hands with Prayer and Anointing at a Celebration of Holy Communion – suitable for use as part of the regular liturgical life of a parish

- Notes on Prayer for Individuals in public worship

- Ministry to the Sick, and Texts for use at the Celebration of Holy Communion with the Sick and Housebound, and at the Distribution of Holy Communion with the Sick and Housebound

- Prayers for Protection and Peace

- Appendices include introductory words, seasonal Bible readings, prayers over the oil, a form of prayer for the laying on of hands with prayer and anointing, and proper prefaces.

A parish service of Wholeness and Healing

This service is designed for occasional use within the regular liturgical life of a parish. The president of the eucharist is assumed also to preside over the ministry of laying on of hands and anointing of the sick, although clearly others can be invited to join in that ministry, if 'authorised'.

It is clear from the notes accompanying Holy Communion Order 1 that the ministry of the whole people of God is expressed through their active participation in the liturgy of the service, and in practical ways throughout the service; for example, in reading, leading intercessions and, with authorisation, assisting at the distribution of Holy Communion. The president draws the congregation into a worshipping community, and maintains the unity of the liturgy. She/he can express that ministry by delegation of part of a service to a deacon, Reader or other episcopally authorised person. Diocesan clarification may be needed in relation to those authorised to pray for wholeness and healing, although it seems likely that local custom and the common sense of the incumbent are paramount.

Some clergy will want to use oil consecrated by the bishop on Maundy Thursday, although within the context of an occasional Wholeness and Healing service in the parish, presidents are encouraged to bless the oil themselves. The formula of consecration echoes the baptismal prayer over the water, and introduces thanksgiving into the heart of the service. A form of prayer is also included for oil previously blessed. The usual place for the laying on of hands and anointing is immediately following the intercessions, although local practice may be followed.

Praying for individuals in public worship

Notes accompanying Wholeness and Healing make it clear that prayer for individuals can take a number of forms including

- prayer for those who do not explain their need or concern

- prayer for those who give a brief explanation of their need to those who will be praying for them

- prayer following an explanation of the person's need to the whole congregation, when that is appropriate.

Those who will be ministering are expected to pray together prior to the service for grace and discernment, having been offered suitable help in preparation for this ministry.

In the context of a communion service, personal ministry may be offered as part of the intercessions, during the distribution of communion, or at the end of the service. However, care should be taken to integrate ministry to individuals with the corporate prayer of the whole church. Prayer for individual needs should not overshadow the gift and promise of communion to the Church.

MARRIAGE

When a couple choose to marry in a church rather than in a civil setting, they are wanting to affirm the place of God in their relationship. More than anything else, the *Common Worship* Marriage Service seeks to encourage that instinct to involve God in marriage. The ASB Marriage service is generally thought of as one of the best in the book, and revision of it has therefore seen few major changes. However, there have been some refinements, and new commended material to resource the authorised liturgy of the service.

The most significant changes in the *Common Worship* Marriage are the division of the service into two halves, the Introduction and the Marriage, and the question addressed to the congregation at the Declaration. The pastoral introduction makes it clear that the congregation are sharing in a journey with the couple, and that by prayer and presence, the support they offer today should also reflect a continuing commitment in the years ahead.

Structure

The division of the service into two parts, the Introduction (including the Liturgy of the Word) and the Marriage (including the prayers and blessing), gives a stronger structure to the whole rite.

Introduction	Welcome
	Preface (replacing the ASB Introduction)
	The Declarations
	The Collect, Reading, and Sermon
The Marriage	Vows
	Giving of Rings
	Proclamation
	Blessing of the Marriage
	Registration
	Prayers and Dismissal

Provision in the notes and appendix include

- The ASB Introduction as an alternative to the *Common Worship* Preface

- The option of 'giving away', with an alternative – a question to the parents of the bride and groom following the Declaration

- Moving the Readings and/or Sermon to a position after the marriage, 'if occasion demands'

- The inclusion of the 'obey' vow in modern language form

- Various alternative vows, prayers, blessings and additional material.

In keeping with the ethos of staged rites and the Christian journey, a service of Thanksgiving for Marriage is included in the commended material accompanying the Pastoral Rites, and could be used, either at home or in church

- On occasions when a number of couples reaffirm their vows together

- To celebrate an anniversary

- After a time of separation or difficulty in marriage.

'Other' or 'others'

The draft of the Marriage Service followed the ASB in changing the wording of the Prayer Book from 'forsaking all other' to 'forsaking all others'. Concern was raised at General Synod, and the service was recommitted to Revision Committee in July 1999. This committee meeting was probably the most expensive piece of liturgical debate in the whole of *Common Worship*! The Revision Committee gathered from around the country to meet for an hour to discuss the 's', and concluded that the medieval Sarum text from which the 1662 Prayer Book took this phrase was plural, thus clearly signifying other men and women, rather than other things.

Christian marriage?

Many couples nowadays want their wedding to reflect something of their own individuality, and it is true that in a marriage service, the couple are their own ministers – until the blessing, the minister acts mostly as a registrar. It is also frequently the case that the regular church congregation do not know the couple, although they will recognise their names from the banns. However, despite all this, if a couple have chosen to marry in church, it is the church's responsibility to provide a liturgy that reflects Christian belief.

The *Common Worship* Marriage Service attempts to update the ASB service and make it relevant to couples marrying in the twenty-first century, while remaining distinctively Christian. For example, the prayers recognise the possibility that one or both partners may already have children. However, it remains to be seen whether the doctrine of the Church as expounded in the 1999 *Marriage* Report of the House of Bishops, and even the ethos behind much of *Common Worship*, will minister successfully to the changing spirituality of twenty-first century England.

FUNERALS

The ASB funeral service reflected the findings of the 1964 Report of the Liturgical Commission on *The Burial of the Dead*. Arguing from a post-Reformation theology, the Report saw the service as performing the following functions

- To secure the reverent disposal of the corpse

- To commend the deceased to the care of our heavenly Father

- To proclaim the glory of our risen life in Christ, here and hereafter

- To remind us of the awful certainty of our own coming death and judgement

- To make plain the eternal unity of God's people, living and departed, in the risen and ascended Christ.

In *Common Worship,* the Liturgical Commission has tried to widen the breadth of its theology, looking at prayer for the departed from the earliest Christian rites, and recognising the pattern of prayer for and about the departed throughout our Christian history. The Pastoral Introduction recognises the humanity of the person who has died (who they were, and what they meant to the mourners), the journey that those present shared with them, and the symbolic role of the rite in allowing expressions of sorrow, faith (or lack of it), and reflection, as part of the process of mourning. The deceased is named throughout the funeral service, and the mourners are prayed for.

The ethos of the Funeral Service

Stronger biblical imagery has been introduced, keeping the ASB emphasis on the resurrection, but strengthening the action of God in the world through the incarnation. The liturgy acts like a lens, bringing into focus the needs, attitudes and beliefs of the mourners in the light of God. There is a recognition of the changing attitude of society to dying and death, and an awareness of the psychological needs of the bereaved; the commended material includes prayers for difficult pastoral situations, both those of the deceased and of the mourners.

The funeral is seen as a stage on a journey, and although the service can stand alone, there is a recognition that prayer may be requested at any point of the process of dying and death. The associated rites include

- Ministry at the time of death

- Before the Funeral – at home (on hearing of someone's death, the evening before), at church (receiving the body, vigil), on the morning of the Funeral

- After the Funeral – at home, the burial of ashes, the Memorial on the Sunday after or at an Annual Memorial.

The importance of an act of commemoration during the church's year is acknowledged, when not only the heroes of the faith, but also our own departed, are remembered. *The Promise of His Glory* included a eucharist for All Souls' Day, 2 November, in commemoration of the faithful departed, and offered a useful introduction to this provision. This service will be included in the forthcoming volume of seasonal resources, *Times and Seasons*.

Structure

The service has six distinctive sections

- Gathering – acknowledging the different groups who come to mourn, and the different stages of grieving. This may include a tribute which acknowledges the life and achievements of the deceased

- Liturgy of the Word – moving the focus from the mourners towards God. The sermon is mandatory and its purpose is to speak about God in the context of the death of the individual

- The Prayers – thanksgiving for the life of the departed, prayer for those who mourn, and prayer for readiness to live in the light of eternity

- Commendation and Farewell

- Committal

- Dismissal.

The notes allow a variety of symbols to be used, including sprinkling the coffin, using a pall, Bible, cross or other symbol, and using the paschal candle. Additional collects, readings and prayers are also included in appendices.

The commended material accompanying the pastoral rites includes a significant number of further resources. These might be chosen to augment the *Common Worship* funeral provision or they could also be used in a more freely devised and constructed funeral using the Outline as the basis of the rite (like A Service of the Word), tailoring a particular service to a particular circumstance, where the normative rite is considered inappropriate.

7
The Christian Year

The *Common Worship* Calendar

The shape of the Christian year is deeply rooted in our tradition, and strongly centred on the Gospel story of *incarnation* and *redemption*.

The *Common Worship* Calendar affirms and clarifies the importance of those two seasons, Christmas and Easter, and the periods of penitence which precede them. The new calendar is also designed to allow the Church of England to join with other churches around the world which are using the *Revised Common Lectionary*.

The most obvious change to the Joint Liturgical Group calendar, as used in the ASB, occurs in the incarnation cycle. The thinking behind the new approach was first presented in *The Promise of His Glory* and is central to the way *Celebrating Common Prayer* celebrates the winter season. The sequence properly begins with Advent Sunday (not five Sundays earlier) and runs to the end of Epiphany, culminating in the Presentation of Christ (Candlemas) on 2 February. This festival, which was once rather ignored, is now an important hinge-point between the incarnation season and the beginning of the passion-resurrection story.

Easter as a season also has more coherence. The whole period from Easter through to Pentecost belongs properly to Eastertide; there is now no suggestion of an 'Ascensiontide'. Again, this is not as new as it seems: *Lent, Holy Week, Easter* directs that the Paschal Candle should remain in its place until the evening of Pentecost, and observes that Ascension Day to Pentecost should be a period during which the Church prays for renewal by the Holy Spirit, rather than a reflection on the ascension itself.

The periods between 3 February and Ash Wednesday, and between Trinity Sunday and the beginning of Advent, are termed 'ordinary time'. These seasons are usually recognised by the use of green as a liturgical colour, and generally have no seasonal emphasis or common theme to the readings.

Apart from the period after Trinity, Sundays are now 'of' a season, rather than Sundays 'after' a Feast, for example, the Third Sunday of Epiphany. In Eastertide this may lead to a little confusion at first, because the familiar numbers of the Eastertide Sundays are altered by one – the Sunday after Easter now being the *second* of the season, since Easter Sunday is the first Sunday in Easter, and so on.

With the emphasis on Pentecost as the culmination of Easter, it would have been inappropriate to continue with 'Sundays after Pentecost'. Instead the BCP title of 'Sundays after Trinity' has been restored.

The Christian year ends with the 'Sundays before Advent', effectively the 'kingdom season' of *Promise* and CCP, though without that title. The suggested liturgical colour is red, though green may be used if preferred. This period begins with the celebration of All Saints' Day and comes to a close with the feast of Christ the King, celebrated on the last Sunday before Advent.

Finally there are some changes to the Calendar of Saints' Days, with an eye to ecumenism, and a considerable number of contemporary names added to the list of commemorations.

The *Common Worship* Lectionary

The lectionary is the way we choose to read the Bible in the course of our corporate worship. The strongly thematic approach of the ASB has been abandoned, and with the *Common Worship* lectionary much more of the scripture is read, often in sequence. The new lectionary is a reworking of the ecumenical *Revised Common Lectionary* (1992), itself a revision of the Roman Catholic *Lectionary for Mass*. The Church of Ireland, the Church in Wales, the Scottish Episcopal Church and the Methodist Church, together with many other churches throughout the world, are also using the RCL. By adopting the RCL, the Church of England immediately opens up to its parishes a great wealth of resources for preachers, those planning and leading worship, and Sunday School teachers. This lectionary is intended for use at the Principal Sunday Service, whether that is a eucharist, Morning Prayer, a baptism, or some other act of worship. The same readings might also be used at an early celebration of Holy Communion on the same day.

The *Common Worship* lectionary also makes provision for a second service, which might typically be used in the evening, and a third service, for churches that need it. Each set of readings complements the others.

Basic principles of the Revised Common Lectionary

- The lectionary has a three-year cycle, each year majoring on one synoptic gospel, which is read continuously (or nearly so) during ordinary time.

- St John's Gospel is read in all three years, particularly during the seasons

- The New Testament readings are not linked to the Gospel of the day; they too are read in sequence

- The Old Testament readings are Gospel-linked in the seasons, but in ordinary time there is a choice of two passages – one track to be read semi-continuously, the other linked to the Gospel

- The psalms are intended to complement the Old Testament reading

- Readings from Acts are preferred to an Old Testament reading in Eastertide, though Old Testament readings are provided for those who require them.

In ordinary time there are no weekly themes or Sunday titles. This has significant implications for the planning of preaching, worship, and music. Preaching is therefore best linked with one particular track of scripture readings for continuity. For example, the preachers may choose to concentrate on the Old Testament reading and the Gospel (if the 'related' track of readings is chosen) or the Old Testament or the New Testament reading. This gives considerable scope for series of sermons examining particular biblical writers or books. In ordinary time it is also permitted to use the lectionary flexibly, so that locally constructed teaching modules might replace some lectionary readings.

Collects and post-communion prayers

A new set of collects has been compiled to complement the new lectionary. They include BCP translations, ASB collects and some new material. There has been a conscious effort to 'marry' the divergent ASB and BCP traditions in the new collects, though arguably this has not been completely successful. Some of them are difficult to pray in certain contexts, particularly those with archaic grammatical structures.

One new feature of the *Common Worship* collects is that during ordinary time, they do not relate to the scripture readings. The sequence of collects and the sequence of readings do not follow each other, and this makes the purchase of a yearly almanac/lectionary almost essential. By contrast, the recent ICEL collects are scripturally related throughout the year. Sadly these are not yet authorised for use in the Church of England.

Common Worship has no seasonal post-communion sentences; instead, there is a fine set of post-communion prayers, which may precede the congregational prayer. These post-communions, some of which are addressed to Christ, explore the paschal mystery in a variety of creative ways.

Seasonal material

When the ASB was published in 1980, it contained more sentences, prayers and readings for holy days and seasons than the Church of England had seen since the Reformation. But it still lagged behind what many churches require. In most parishes, Advent is celebrated with a ring of candles and a crib is blessed at Christmas; many also bless a Paschal Candle and celebrate an Easter Vigil; yet none of this is provided for in the Prayer Book or the ASB. Neither is there any provision for Carol Services in Advent or at Christmas, prayers for Christian Unity in Epiphany, or services on Ash Wednesday or during Holy Week.

Lent, Holy Week, Easter (1986) and its companion volume *The Promise of His Glory* (1991) go a very long way to meet these needs and have been warmly welcomed as fine enrichments to the services in the ASB. It might seem at first sight that these books do not quite belong with *Common Worship*, but in fact they strongly share its ethos of seasonal enrichment around a common core. These volumes, along with other seasonal material, are due to be published in a revised and expanded form within the next two years; but in the meantime, both books can continue to be used, with appropriate adaptation to responses and so on, to complement *Common Worship*.

Lent, Holy Week, Easter and *The Promise of His Glory* contain three kinds of resources. Firstly, there are complete services for particular occasions, like Palm Sunday, Good Friday, All Souls' Day, Christmas Morning and so on. Secondly, there is resource material for enriching *Common Worship* services: prayers, canticles, intercessions, sentences to introduce the confession and the peace, blessings and other resources. Thirdly, both contain alternative lectionaries, which were, in effect, early versions of the *Common Worship* lectionary; these are now obsolete.

Alongside these should be placed *Patterns for Worship* (1995), which also contains a great deal of seasonal material. The House of Bishops has commended all three volumes without any time limit, and unless the diocesan bishop has given other directions, parishes can therefore freely use them all.

In addition to these books of commended material, there is a growing body of unofficial resources, which can be used wherever 'other suitable words' are suggested. They are not, of course, exhaustive; most ministers draft suitable words of their own as well! But they are an invaluable treasure-trove of ideas, and often provide a good starting point for something else. Probably the best known and most useful is

Michael Perham's *Enriching the Christian Year*, which draws on existing authorised and commended material as well as introducing new texts. More suggestions can be found in the bibliography at the end of this book.

Using seasonal resources in the parish

Perhaps the best use of the books on offer is to incorporate a selection of their material in locally produced booklets. There is far too much seasonal material to include it all in each booklet, so careful choices have to be made each time. Whether the services and prayers are used this way, or whether 'presidential' prayers are simply imported into existing services by worship leaders, the general expectation nowadays is that the parish priest will work closely with a parish worship team to make sensitive, informed and shared decisions about what is needed.

8

Resourcing *Common Worship*

It will be clear by now that *Common Worship* services are written to allow a high degree of flexibility, and that to make best use of them will demand a great deal from all those involved in planning and leading worship. In many ways the most important resource – apart from the texts themselves – is the liturgical awareness, creativity and sensitivity of ministers, parish worship teams and congregations working together.

One way to celebrate the *Common Worship* liturgies would be to buy the main book and the book of pastoral offices, and simply follow the texts printed there. Even *that* will require thought and preparation, to say nothing of getting congregations used to new responses and prayers. But of course, many parishes will want to do a much better job than that, and will wish to make full use of the new provisions. They will want to tailor the liturgy to their own local needs; they may want to produce seasonal service booklets for the main Sunday services; and they will want to make sure that the pastoral offices can be celebrated with due respect for the people concerned.

LOCALLY PRODUCED SERVICE BOOKS

Although the eucharist can be celebrated in a wide variety of ways, most churches tend to have a settled way of doing things, and might benefit from using local service booklets that set this out clearly. Imagine two fictional churches ...

At St Anne's, the confession is always used at the beginning of the service and the congregation are used to a Kyrie form. The vicar is so fond of eucharistic prayer B that he hardly ever uses anything else. Because the church is part of a Local Ecumenical Project, they also use the ecumenical form of the Lord's Prayer, and need a rubric that makes it clear that members of other churches are welcome to receive communion here. The parish worship team have therefore decided to produce their own booklet, effectively 'Order 1 at St Anne's'. It gives worshippers a clear path through the liturgy without the priest constantly having to call out page numbers and jump around the service book.

Down the road at St Tobias's, the PCC have recently discovered the wealth of material available to celebrate the Church's seasons. Their new vicar frequently uses prayers from *The Promise of His Glory* and *Lent, Holy Week, Easter*, and she's been saying for months that she wishes the whole congregation could join in some of these prayers and responsories. In a sudden flurry of activity, the worship team have produced a set of service booklets for Advent, Christmas, Ordinary Time, Lent, and Eastertide. They are particularly pleased with their Advent booklet. It begins with the lighting of the Advent candles and has a wonderfully seasonal feel to the penitential prayers, the intercession, the peace, post-communion prayers and blessing. They chose to print eucharistic prayer E with one of the long Advent prefaces. The congregation are pleased to have all these texts in their hands, as well as on the priest's prayer-desk. The worship team enjoyed working with the priest to choose the prayers, and the Sunday School children drew pictures to illustrate the new booklets.

Where to begin

Attractive and professional-looking service booklets are not difficult to produce. The starting point is, of course, the service itself. All worship in the Church of England must be from an authorised source, which, with a few exceptions, now means either *Common Worship* or the 1662 Prayer Book. On specific occasions, for example Palm Sunday or Christmas morning, services commended by the House of Bishops from *Lent, Holy Week, Easter* or *The Promise of His Glory* may be used.

Authorised services can always be supplemented with prayers and other material from the seasonal books mentioned above, or from other commended material like *Patterns for Worship.* Other, 'unofficial' resources can be freely used wherever the service allows 'other suitable words'. So, for example, the intercessions and seasonal canticles from books like *Enriching the Christian Year* will be helpful, or suitable texts might be composed locally.

All this means that the basic shape of the service, and most of the texts, are already given, albeit with a great deal of freedom to adapt and supplement services with a rich variety of other material. The task of the worship team producing a local service booklet is to draw together all these elements of liturgical tradition in creative ways which enable the congregation to enter more deeply into the mystery of the Christian story.

Preparing the text

Once the text is agreed, it needs to be set out and printed. The minimum requirement to produce service books 'in-house' is

- a computer system running a good word processor or desktop publishing package, with a modern laser or inkjet printer

- an electronic version of the text (see below)

- access to a scan-printer, high-volume photocopier or some other duplicating facility.

There are several formats in which a service might be produced, including the 'concertina' cards favoured by CHP for the initiation services in 1998. For most parishes, however, the choice will be between a booklet of 8, 12 or 16 A5 pages with a card cover; or a simple fold-over A4 card. A booklet gives scope to print presidential and ministerial texts (like the eucharistic prayer) in full, and will allow an uncluttered layout. A card, on the other hand, is cheaper to produce and easier to use, but will only allow enough room for congregational texts and some ministerial 'lead-ins'.

Electronic text

There are many ways to get the text of a service into your word processor. Typing it in is usually a bad idea, if only because of the risk of typographical mistakes. A much better approach is to obtain the text from an official source. All *Common Worship* services are available for download from the website from November 2000. However, for much greater flexibility and power, it is worth considering buying the computer program *Visual Liturgy*. This contains the text of all the *Common Worship* services, the words of many hymns (though not those still subject to copyright), and the collects, readings and post-communions for the Principal Service in both NIV and NRSV versions of the Bible. An add-on *Seasonal Module* includes most of *Lent, Holy Week and Easter*, *The Promise of his Glory* and *Patterns for Worship*, as well as some material from *Enriching the Christian Year*.

Visual Liturgy is far more than a repository of texts. Using this software, it is possible to tailor an order of service to almost anyone's needs, and to search for any prayer contained within its vast database within seconds. It has an integrated ecclesiastical calendar, making it possible to import collects and readings with ease. *Visual Liturgy* will also record the usage of hymns and do much more besides.

Once your service order has been fine-tuned in *Visual Liturgy*, it can be exported to another application to be laid out properly on the page.

The *Visual Liturgy* website is at www.vislit.com

Copyright

The reproduction of copyright material can be a complex matter, since each copyright holder is entitled to place such conditions on the use of their work as they see fit.

However with *Common Worship* and other authorised and commended material in the Church of England, there are special arrangements which simplify the procedure greatly. There is no need to apply for copyright permission or pay a fee, provided that the booklets are not sold, the name of the parish is clearly displayed, no more than 500 copies are made and copyright is acknowledged in the proper way.

Common Worship services from the main book should be acknowledged as follows

> Common Worship: Services and Prayers for the Church of England, *material from which is included in this service, is copyright © The Archbishops' Council 2000.*

Copyright of material from other authorised or commended sources is acknowledged in the same way, with suitable alteration to the wording.

Any parish wishing to use texts from other sources must abide by the wishes of the copyright holder and, where required, seek their permission directly. For example, material from *Enriching the Christian Year* may be reproduced for use on a single occasion or annually, but more frequent use requires a written application.

It should go without saying that churches will respect the law and the legal rights of copyright holders, and refrain from reproducing copyright texts without permission.

A full statement of the position can be found in *A Brief Guide to Liturgical Copyright*, which is available both in print and at www.cofe.anglican.org/commonworship

Some do's and don'ts

Care and thought needs to be given to the production of the booklets. For example

* What kind of service is it for? A family service has a very different 'feel' from a confirmation, and the service books/cards should reflect that.

* What rubrics (instructions) are necessary? It may be that very few are needed, but local customs may need pointing out.

- Are the page breaks in sensible places, avoiding strange breaks in the middle of prayers? (The ASB had a spectacularly bad one between pages 131 and 132.)

- Is the combination of typeface and point-size readable, remembering that some worshippers have difficulty reading small print? It may in any case be worth producing a few copies in large print.

- How many fonts have been used? There should usually be two at most – one for liturgical text, and perhaps another for headings and rubrics.

- Is it clear who says which texts? The use of **bold** type for texts said together is now so well established that it should be unnecessary to mark congregational texts with the word 'All' in the left margin.

- Is there plenty of white space on each page? Cramped texts can look dreadful and be difficult to read.

- Has a suitable copyright acknowledgement been made, and permission sought where necessary (see above)?

There are plenty of good, stylish examples around to copy – and some poor ones to avoid! A model of good liturgical printing is the 1982 eucharistic rite of the Scottish Episcopalian Church. The booklet is gloriously economical with both text and rubric, and lays out the service with beauty and clarity.

If you are producing copies in large print, remember too to print an altar copy. Pages can be placed in A4 display books, and are a *much* cheaper alternative to the CHP book of altar services, unless the musical and other resources in that book will be of benefit to your church.

MUSIC

For many churches, the change in liturgy is an opportunity to look afresh at worship as a whole. Unfortunately, musical resources for *Common Worship* are still sparse at the time of writing. Most parishes will be able to continue using their current Communion settings, with slight modifications for the *Common Worship* word changes.

The Royal School of Church Music (RSCM) is publishing a Resource Book of Eucharistic settings, both old and new, grouped by texts, such as the Kyries, the Gloria, the Creed, etc. Settings for all eight eucharistic prayers, including the congregational acclamations, are included. The Resource Book also includes responses and canticles for the Offices, and examples of different ways to sing the Psalms. The Institute for Liturgy and Mission at Sarum College have produced useful booklets on musical accompaniments to Holy Communion, Initiation, and A Service of the Word.

A useful resource for those choosing hymns to go with the lectionary is *Sing His Glory*, Canterbury Press, 1997. Those affiliated to the RSCM receive, with the quarterly newsletter *Sunday by Sunday*, a weekly guide for those who plan and lead services. This gives a biblical commentary, followed by suggestions for hymns and songs taken from a very wide range of books, with ideas for Psalm settings, anthems, and organ music. Occasional articles and musical ideas supplement this basic material.

A complete musical resource using the *Common Worship* Psalter has yet to appear, but there are a number of collections of Psalms available. These are included in the Bibliography, under Resources for A Service of the Word.

INTRODUCING *COMMON WORSHIP* IN THE PARISH

The following letter has been used to good effect in Durham Diocese as an introduction to the liturgical changes. A version of it could be sent by clergy to members of the electoral roll, printed in the parish magazine, or given out to the congregation with the notice sheet. It could also include information about Morning and Evening Prayer on Sunday, and the use of local service books. If the parish has a worship team, this may be a good opportunity to encourage the work of that group, and to develop thinking about future shared ministry.

You may freely use this letter in your own parish, either as it is, or in an altered form. However, if you add texts from *Common Worship* services, you should include a proper copyright acknowledgement (see above).

Common Worship

Advent marks the beginning of the Christian Year, and we are marking Advent 2000 by introducing Common Worship, the services that the Church of England is introducing for the new century. Common Worship replaces the ASB, and we will be saying more about the new liturgy in sermons, but I have also decided to give you the main points in writing so that everyone on the electoral roll is as clear as can be about what is happening.

At this church, like many in the country, we have already made a start to this changeover, by using the Common Worship Calendar, Lectionary, and Collects, and the baptism service. Now the time has come to change our regular

Sunday Communion Services. Most of the prayers and responses haven't changed, but at four points in the service responses that we may know by heart have been slightly altered, and these may trip us up. The old words 'fellow men' in the confession have changed to the more biblical word 'neighbours', recalling Jesus' command to love God and our neighbour. I have printed the new texts of the Gospel Responses, the Creed, and the Opening Sentences of the eucharistic prayer below ...

There has been considerable debate in the Church of England about the Lord's Prayer, and three versions are given as alternatives in Common Worship. The English-speaking churches throughout the world have agreed an ecumenical version which is included, along with the Church of England's independent translation, and the traditional version. During the coming months, the PCC will be giving some thought to the version that we use here, so to help us all to start to think about it, I have also printed the ecumenical version of the Lord's Prayer below ...

I believe that the changeover to Common Worship will prove a good experience for this church, bringing freshness to our worship, and new riches to our prayers. As we have drawn our liturgy from the traditions and faith of Christians through the centuries, so now we play our own part in shaping the tradition of Anglican worship for today and for the future.

Appendix A
Bibliography

The publications listed below are divided into categories for convenience, but many are valuable resources in more than one area. Some were not yet published as this book went to press, but they should all be available by early 2001.

HOLY COMMUNION

The Eucharistic Prayers of Order One
Colin Buchanan & Charles Read
Grove Worship Series 158, 2000

The New Eucharistic Rite: Order One
Jeremy Fletcher
Grove Worship Series 159, 2000

Praxis Communion Services Training Pack
Praxis Resources
Sarum College, 19 The Close, Salisbury, SP1 2EE

Music Resources for *Common Worship* Eucharist
Robert Fielding
Sarum College, 19 The Close, Salisbury, SP1 2EE

Sing His Glory: *Hymns for the three year lectionary*
Canterbury Press, 1998

Using *Common Worship* Holy Communion
Mark Beach,
Church House Publishing/Praxis, 2000

A SERVICE OF THE WORD

A Service of the Word
Trevor Lloyd
Grove Worship Series 151, 1999

Patterns for Worship
Church House Publishing, 1995

Enriching the Christian Year
Ed. Michael Perham
SPCK, 1993

Lent, Holy Week, Easter: *Services and Prayers*
Church House Publishing, 1986

The Promise of His Glory
Church House Publishing, 1991

Opening Prayers: *Scripture-related collects
for Years A, B & C*
Canterbury Press, 1999

Music Resources for *Common Worship*
A Service of the Word
Robert Fielding
Sarum College, 19 The Close, Salisbury, SP1 2EE

MUSICAL RESOURCES

Psalm Songs 1, 2, & 3: *responsorial settings of song-like psalm paraphrases, with some ICEL and Grail texts*
Cassell, 1998

Psalms and Music for the Eucharist: *responsorial psalms from lectionary Year A*
McCrimmonds, 1998
It is regrettable that the publisher has decided not to publish Years B & C

Sunday Psalms: *responsorial settings of the NRSV Psalms in numerical order*
Kevin Mayhew, 1998

A series of Psalms for the RCL
Redemptorist Publications
Alphonsus House, Chawton, Hants, GU34 3HQ

Common Praise
The successor to Hymns Ancient and Modern
Canterbury Press, 2000

INITIATION SERVICES

On the Way: *Towards an Integrated Approach to Christian Initiation*
Church House Publishing, 1995

Praxis Initiation Services Training Pack
Praxis Resources
Sarum College, 19 The Close, Salisbury, SP1 2EE

New Initiation Rites
Colin Buchanan & Michael Vasey
Grove Worship Series 145, 1998

Baptism Matters
Nick and Hazel Whitehead
Church House Publishing, 1998

Music Resources for *Common Worship* Initiation
Robert Fielding
Sarum College, 19 The Close, Salisbury, SP1 2EE

Using *Common Worship* Baptism
Gilly Myers
Church House Publishing/Praxis, 2000

PASTORAL SERVICES

***Common Worship* Wholeness and Healing**
Colin Buchanan
Grove Worship Series 161, 2000

Revising Weddings
Charles Read
Grove Worship Series 128, 1994

***Common Worship* Funerals**
Trevor Lloyd
Grove Worship Series 158, 2000

Prayer and the Departed
Chris Cocksworth
Grove Worship Series 142, 1997

Praxis Pastoral Services Training Pack
Praxis Resources
Sarum College, 19 The Close, Salisbury, SP1 2EE

Using *Common Worship* Marriage
Steven Lake
Church House Publishing/Praxis, 2000

Using *Common Worship* Funerals
Ann Horton
Church House Publishing/Praxis, 2000

A New Handbook of Pastoral Liturgy
Michael Perham
SPCK, 2000

THE CHRISTIAN YEAR

See also A SERVICE OF THE WORD

Introducing the New Lectionary
Lloyd, Moger, Sinclair, and Vasey
Grove Worship Series 141, 1997

Celebrate the Christian Story
Michael Perham
SPCK, 1997

Praxis Lectionary Training Pack
Praxis Resources
Sarum College, 19 The Close, Salisbury, SP1 2EE

Exciting Holiness: *Collects and Readings for Festivals and Lesser Festivals*
Ed. Brother Tristam SSF
Canterbury Press, 1997

Celebrating the Saints: *Daily spiritual readings for the Calendar of the Church of England*
Robert Atwell
Canterbury Press, 1998

Celebrating the Seasons: *Daily spiritual readings for the Christian Year*
Robert Atwell
Canterbury Press, 1999

INTRODUCING *COMMON WORSHIP*

Towards Liturgy 2000
Ed. Michael Perham
SPCK/Alcuin, 1989

Liturgy for a New Century
Ed. Michael Perham
SPCK/Alcuin, 1991

***Common Worship* Today**
GROW, Harper Collins, 2000

A Companion to *Common Worship*
Ed. Paul Bradshaw
SPCK, 2001

A Brief Guide to Liturgical Copyright
Church House Publishing, October 1997

Producing Your Own Orders of Service
Mark Earey
Church House Publishing, 2000

Appendix B
Glossary of Terms

ablutions	consuming the bread and wine remaining after holy communion, and cleaning the vessels
acclamation	a congregational response, often of praise, to a ministerial prayer or sentence
Agnus Dei	Latin for 'Lamb of God', a song used either during or after the breaking of bread at the eucharist
anamnesis	(1) 'remembrance' or 'memorial' – in this sense, the whole eucharistic preface is an anamnesis (2) the section of the eucharistic prayer that links the offering or 'doing' of the eucharist to the recalling of the life, death and resurrection of Christ
ASB	Alternative Service Book, authorised for use 1980-2000
authorised liturgy	services or prayers authorised by the General Synod either for a limited period or until further resolution of the Synod – these may be used freely by any parish
BCP	1662 *Book of Common Prayer*

Benedictus Latin for 'blessed' – the song 'Blessed is he who comes ...'

bidding a short prayer, usually followed by silence and a congregational response

canticle a song of praise (or sometimes of lament or penitence), normally taken verbatim from scripture

CCP *Celebrating Common Prayer* (Anglican Franciscan Daily Prayer)

collect (a) a compact prayer which ends a litany or period of silent prayer
(b) the prayer which concludes the opening part of the eucharist, often related to the readings of the day

commended liturgy services or prayers commended by the House of Bishops – these may be used by any parish unless the diocesan bishop has directed otherwise

deacon (a) a person ordained to the office of a deacon
(b) at the eucharist, the person taking the assistant's role (see chapter 3)

ecumenical churches of different denominations working together; concerning all Christian churches

ECUSA Episcopal Church of the United States of America

ELLC	English Language Liturgical Consultation (ecumenical)
epiclesis	the invocation (calling down) of the Holy Spirit on the gifts or on the worshippers at the eucharist
ICEL	International Commission on English in the Liturgy (Roman Catholic)
inclusive language	language which avoids gender-specific words such as 'fellow men', or is all-encompassing, for example 'sisters and brothers'
institution narrative	the recitation of the words and actions of Jesus at the Last Supper when he 'instituted' the eucharist
JLG	Joint Liturgical Group (ecumenical)
Kyrie eleison	Greek for 'Lord, have mercy', a set of penitential sentences at the beginning of the eucharist; often abbreviated to kyrie
litany	a set of short prayers, each of which is followed by a congregational response
liturgy	literally, 'the work of the people'; the worship of the people of God, particularly the words, hymns and songs of services

memorial acclamation	a section of the anamnesis in which the congregation join, in words recalling the death and resurrection of Christ
ministerial text	text or prayer spoken by one of the ministers alone
oblation	the part of the eucharistic prayer concerned with offering
opening dialogue	the three responsive couplets at the beginning of the eucharistic prayer
paschal	concerning Easter; concerning the death and resurrection of Christ
pastoral offices	services for times of pastoral need, particularly wholeness and healing, marriage and funerals. Baptism and confirmation are sometimes called 'pastoral offices' too, but in the *Common Worship* provision they are grouped as Initiation services
post-communion	the prayer(s) said after communion by the president, usually in collect form
preface	the part of the eucharistic prayer between the opening dialogue and the Sanctus, recalling the mighty acts of God in thanksgiving
president	the priest or bishop who 'presides' over the service; the word is normally used at the eucharist

presidential text	text or prayer spoken by the presiding minister alone
principal service	the main service on a Sunday or feast day, whether the eucharist, Morning Prayer, A Service of the Word, or some other act of worship
RCL	Revised Common Lectionary
RSCM	Royal School of Church Music
rubric	an instruction as to how a part of the liturgy is to be celebrated
Sanctus	Latin for 'holy' – the song 'Holy, holy, holy Lord ...'
1928 Prayer Book	the first attempt at liturgical change since the seventeenth century, which was never officially authorised. Parts of it nevertheless came into general use, with the blessing of the bishops